# Wattle and Wagtails

Susan Skowronski

BookLeaf Publishing

India | USA | UK

Presentation by *BookLeaf Publishing*

Web: www.bookleafpub.com

E-mail: info@bookleafpub.com


ISBN: 9789358314335

First edition 2023

# DEDICATION

Dedicated to my husband Victor whose love
and support inspires me and makes my dreams
come true

# Wagtail

WAGTAIL

Chittering chattering
chirping rattling
restless strutting,
tail flicking side to side
little David meets Goliath
fierce aggressor, brave defender
the wagtail stands his ground
mocks his vanquished foe

# Wattle

Wattle by my window
a vibrant splash of gold
such bold exuberance
defies the winter chill

All around the trees are bare
the day is bleak and cold

In the absence of the sun's rays
the wattle gives its all
scents the air with fragrance
adds colour to the garden
brings a sense of joy

# Suburban Dawn

Butcher birds' chorus
greets the approaching dawn
high in the flowering gum
a kookaburra joins in

Willie wagtail's
sweet repetitive song
'Which are you, Willie
which are you?'
floats over sleeping houses

Lorikeets chittering
strident and shrill
peewee pair perform
a wing-lifting duet
dove cooing gently
flirts with his mate
the day has begun!

# Sunrise in the Wetlands

Mist-filtered rays
 of the rising sun
create an atmosphere…
an expectation
of the Light to come

In an overhanging she-oak
a kingfisher watches intently
Welcome swallows begin
their swooping patrols
over the lake

Dragonflies hover
over pink waterlilies
boronias
and yellow marsh flowers
Praise God for this morning

# Full Moon

Billabong shimmering in the moonlight
paperbarks rustle
she-oaks whisper
a gentle breeze carries
sweet perfume of boronias
tang of lemon scented gum
Away to the North
a lone dingo calls
distant, long and sorrowful howl
Answered…
in the scrub nearby…

Too close for comfort!
I turn away
return to camp.

# Tawny Frogmouth

A broken branch
slowly morphs -
a frogmouth revealed

Yellow eyes gaze intently
No warning hiss
no snapping beak
no threat perceived
no attempt to flee

Our eyes lock
Moments pass in silence
communicating mutual respect

He turns away
becomes a branch
safe in the ironbark

# Egret

Poised bride-like
slender body elegant in snowy white
her lacy veil
cascading
across folded wings
lifting lightly in a gentle breeze

She waits
motionless
expectant in the shallows

# Wompoo Encounter

At the edge of the rainforest
On a hot summer afternoon
the stillness is broken
by a deep throated call
powerful, reverberating -
'wallock-a-woo'

High in the canopy
a flash of purple and grey
a Wompoo fruit dove
enjoying the figs
'wallock-a-woo'
such spectacular colours
he doesn't seem real

I gaze up in wonder
my spirits revived
my Wompoo encounter
on that hot afternoon

# Firefly

Moonlight reflects on the water
wattle scents mingle with
woodsmoke drifting skyward
Fishermen wait in hope
A willie wagtail serenades
A lone firefly blinks its way
along the bank
approaches my campfire
pauses a moment
then continues on its way

# Solace

Colours of sunset
slowly fade to grey
lorikeets settle
twitterings cease
wagtail flicks his tail
and flies away to roost

The evening star appears
before the moon has risen
before the possums scavenge
before the owls begins to hunt

Lemon scented myrtle
fresh sweet eucalyptus
the heady scent of wattle
carried on the breeze

I sense a gentle presence
a caress upon my cheek
a whisper in the darkness
brings the solace that I seek

# Claret Ash

Claret ash stark and bare
against a grey winter's sky -
the splendour of Autumn
forgotten
last leaf released
to flutter away
become lost
in the leaf litter carpet

 A babbler's nest
firmly clutched by
the uppermost branches
predicts spring's return
brings hope for new life
on a cold winter's day

# Gloaming

Rose pink light
at the end of the day
drains away colour
softens the landscape
creates silhouettes
and darkening shadows.

She-oaks whisper
in the slight evening breeze
invite home coming birds
to seek shelter and roost,
bring peace to the lakeside
and welcome the night.

The stillness of gloaming –
a moment to pause
give thanks for the day
and labours' rewards.

Serenity creeps in
grants farmlands their rest

# Jacaranda Dreaming

Old man
beneath the jacaranda
dreams of a long ago love

Blossoms surround him
enchant him
one like a butterfly
alights on his hand
delicate fragrance evokes a memory
of love's first shy kiss.

She danced on tip toe
in a purple-blue dress
on a carpet of blossoms
weaving her spell

The old man
closes his eyes
and begins to dance.

# Camellia

Camellias after rain
blanketing paths and lawns
exquisite in their spent life
their death a gift of beauty
a soft fragrant carpet
to delight passing feet

Lingering raindrops reflect the morning sun
glisten, give brief new life
to fallen flowers
a thanksgiving for their sacrifice

# OLIVES

Sunlight filters through
branches of the olive tree
weighed down with bitter fruit,
inedible now,
but soaked in brine
tomorrow's gourmet feast.

In my secret shady bower
I ponder on these ancient truths -
the taste of salt
peace and loyalty
and olive branches.

A peaceful dove alights nearby
enters my safe haven
and coos gently in my ear.

# Thornbill

Afternoon sunlight
tints tawny branches
a gentle breeze
stirs fresh new leaves
as lingering blossoms fall
to drift across the garden.

Cheeky little thornbills
seen…unseen…and seen again
a flash of brown and yellow
flits among spring flowers
delight us with their song

# Journeying Westward

Journeying westward
a shimmering black river
snaking towards the horizon

Tumbleweed rolling
          rushing
                    scurrying
dodges speeding trucks
dawdling caravans
occasional roo.


Wedgetail abandons its feast
          rises slowly
          languid and graceful
on powerful wings
glides towards the sun

# Wedgetail

Communing with the gods,
circling aloft
above the sunbaked earth
without effort
not even a wingbeat -
but ever alert.

Magnificent magnifying eye
maps every move
every twitch
every breath
of creatures below.
The wedgetail sees them all.

Apex predator
of Australian plains
swift and straight
drops to prey

# Campfire

Huddled by the campfire,
sipping a glass of red
cocooned in our little world of firelight
wrapped in darkness
intense and mysterious
a world apart.

A possum on an overhanging branch
a thousand twinkling stars above
the hoot of an owl unseen
a wagtail's serenade
remind us we are free
to dream
to leave reality behind
enjoy a moment
when we are not ruled by
the chaos of our everyday life.

# Flame Tree

Flame tree
ablaze in the driveway
heralds the Christmas Season

No tinsel, no baubles
Nature's beauty supreme
expression of joy

A myriad tiny red bells
festoon each branch.
Fallen flowers
embellish gardens
and transform pathways

Red carpet welcome –
come and celebrate!

# Scent from the Patio

A sweet once-familiar scent
drifts in from the patio
evoking memories
of evening companionship
after dinner conversation
amusing stories of your day
thoughts from the past
hope for the future
old cane chairs with threadbare cushions
clouds sweeping across a moonlit sky.

I close my eyes
and breathe deeply.
You're not here
but our tobacco plant is blooming again

9 789358 314335